I Love !
You .

THE MAGIC WORD

Revised Edition

W.D. GANN

Foreword

Everyone who writes a book has some definite aim or objective. Some write to relieve pent-up emotions, some for financial gain, others for fame and ambition; but the writer who does the greatest good for his readers and for himself is the man who writes with a sincere desire to help others. The greatest good that we can do for others is to show them how to help themselves when they are ready and want assistance, and to make them independent instead of dependent. The man who can render helpful service to others is a success and enjoys happiness and peace of mind through giving the best he has.

The objective in writing *The Magic Word* is to show others the way to use and obey God's Divine Law and thus help them to bring out their latent talents and their God-given powers, for that is the only way they can realize health, happiness and prosperity.

I write with the knowledge that I have already received many blessings by applying the Magic Word and give thanks for the rewards I have received and shall hope to receive from my efforts in trying to help others. When they find the way through the Magic Word to a realization of their hopes and desires they will bless me for directing them in the right path. I feel certain millions of people will read The Magic Word and benefit by it.

Introduction to
THE MAGIC WORD

The Bible teaches a divine law and how you can make it work. It teaches two things: Obedience to the law brings reward; disobedience to the law brings punishment. The Good Book does not say that you have to wait until after death to receive a reward. What people want are health, happiness and prosperity here and now on this earth, not a promise of something received after they are dead. This is a practical religion and the Magic Word, ALMIGHTY, will teach you how to get what you need - here and now!

What The Magic Word Does For You

There is power in the word ALMIGHTY. The word ALMIGHTY gives you life, renewed energy and health.
The Magic Word, ALMIGHTY, is the truth, and the truth will set you free. The word is what removes all doubts and fears.
Do not just listen to the word; instead, put it into practice. If you listen to the word but do not put it into practice, you are like people who look in a mirror and see themselves as they are. They take a good look at themselves and then go away and immediately forget what they look like.

You must put The Magic Word, ALMIGHTY, into action. Knowing the word and not doing will not get results. You must continue to repeat and concentrate on the word.

The word for which such great search has been made and which so many people expect to be so far from them is actually in their hearts and in their mouths. All that you need to do to get health, happiness and wealth is TO USE THE WORD ALMIGHTY: SPEAK IT, ACT IT, PRAY WITH IT, AND MEDITATE AND CONCENTRATE ON IT. You must learn to speak the Magic Word, ALMIGHTY, at the time and place given in another chapter. If you do this with faith your reward is certain, as promised in the Bible.

The word ALMIGHTY conveys the oneness of the ONE GOD who is fixed and permanent. It was powerful and worked miracles in the old days and is just as powerful and will work miracles today, if you believe and put it into action. You can test it for yourself by following the laws and rules written in the Bible, get results and learn that it works today.

The MAGIC WORD will bring you a realization of all your desires.

The aim of this book is to prove the value of the Magic Word by the Bible, and not to give the writer's opinion or the writer's rules. You can obtain results and prove to yourself that these divine laws work. The objective of this book is to prove to you what the divine word is and give you the evidence of how to use the Magic Word, ALMIGHTY, to obtain health, happiness and prosperity.

Everything is in the Bible for you to use to obtain all the aims and objectives throughout life, by working through the divine word, ALMIGHTY.

Among the best books of the Bible to read are: Psalms, Proverbs and Songs of Solomon, but you should use a Bible with a concordance and read everything under faith, fasting, love, prayer, spirit, truth, peace, forgiveness, anger, jealousy, hate, evil thoughts, money, prosperity, sacrifice, selfishness, self-denial, charity and patience.

The Bible is the greatest book ever written and contains the truth and the solution to all your problems. When you learn, understand, obey and apply the laws revealed in the Bible, you can overcome all your troubles, physical as well as financial. Let us pay reverence to this great Book and proceed to seek the light that will lead us out of darkness and eradicate fear, giving us faith, hope and confidence based on the knowledge of the law.

How can truth and knowledge eliminate fear and make us free? When we are possessed with fear, doubt and worry, we waste our energy by retarding and limiting our possibilities of obtaining our desires. We fear and worry because we do not know. When we need money, we worry and fear that we will not get it. When we are sick, we fear that we will not get well. But when we have knowledge of the divine law of supply and demand and know how to draw upon the universal laws, which supply all our desires, then are we free from fear and worry. Therefore, let us proceed with an open mind to face and seek the truth, the divine law and the magic word of power; find it and be free.

Knock at the door of knowledge, believing that it will be opened to you and don't stop seeking and knocking until you have received. THE MAGIC WORD will teach you the law. Obey the law and nothing will be impossible. But do not overlook the fact that you cannot get something good for nothing and that what is worth having is worth praying and working for. Only your own returns to you; you must give to receive. Everything is yours if you pay the price for it, so after you know how to use the MAGIC WORD, you must work for the desired results.

To work without faith and knowledge of the Divine Law and the MAGIC WORD will not get results. *You must know what you want; know the divine law whereby you can get it, obey the law, have patience and work until you succeed.*

Start to read this course of instructions with the faith that there is no limit to the divine power of the MAGIC WORD and realize that you are a part of the divine creative power and will find your Master in yourself. Your Master's voice will be heard through the MAGIC WORD. Then sickness, poverty, doubt, worry, fear, envy, jealousy and death will disappear. You will find what you have been seeking. Your heart will be filled with joy and your life brimming with love and happiness through the light and use of the MAGIC WORD.

Chapter I

HISTORY OF THE MAGIC WORD OR LOST WORD

Long before the pyramids of Egypt, men sought the "Philosopher's Stone," a magic stone by which he might turn all metals into gold. Likewise, men have sought the Lost Word, the possession of which they believed would give them all power and bring them all good things in life to help them gain money, happiness and financial independence.

In ancient times it was generally believed that the Jews possessed the WORD but that they in some way lost it. A near lifelong search for the Lost Word was made by Reuchlin of Germany. Pico Della Mirondola, in Italy, devoted his lifetime to a search for the Lost Word.

Refer to Amos 8:12: -- "People will wander from the Dead Sea to the Mediterranean and then on around from the north to the east. They will look everywhere for a message from the Lord, but they will not find it." This is further proof that there was a word which was secret for a time, and those who did not use it in the right way were not permitted to know it.

The fact that men have sought so long to find the Lost Word proves that there must have been a Word of Power in the past. Otherwise, men would not have spent a lifetime trying to find it. If there is some good proof or evidence from past history that such a word existed and was lost - probably through the fall or disobedience of man - then it certainly exists today. If it does, it has just as great power today as it ever had before it was lost.

The Bible tells what the Divine Word of Power is. The purpose of this book is to show you how to find and use the word of power or the *Magic Word*.

Chapter II

THE WORD ALMIGHTY

In Psalms 68:4 we are told to sing praises unto God's name and rejoice before him. You will get excellent results using the word ALMIGHTY, or you may use the name God, Lord or Israel, all depending upon the keynote, or musical sound or tone, that will start the proper vibrations in your body to produce harmony.

THE SPOKEN WORD IS VERY IMPORTANT. Some people cannot heal themselves by speaking the word themselves, but when they hear others speak it, they learn from them and have faith in others while they do not have faith in themselves. If you understand the Magic Word and know that you have it in you, you can ask what you will and it will be done for you.

God's sacred name and the divine word ALMIGHTY is the Magic Word of truth. You will no longer doubt, fear or hate after you know the truth and speak the Word, for knowing the truth and speaking the Word will make you free.

To meet the Lord in the air and be ever with the Lord, means breathing in the air or speaking into the air the word ALMIGHTY. Then when you repeat the word ALMIGHTY, the Magic Word, your message goes into the air and you have met the Lord in the air, and if you continue to speak the Word into the air you can expect the Word to be returned to you, fulfilled.

We read in God's Word that he will give to us according to our work; that he will bless those who keep his commandments. He admonishes us to reverence His name, pray in silence and not to talk too much. When you talk too much you give out your energy, your strength and your secrets. The ancients claimed that what you retained for your own must be kept within yourself.

There is an old saying that a thing talked about continually never happens. People who talk much or make plans but never execute them do not get any results. You will accomplish more by silently working with the Word and obeying the law.

In Numbers, Chapter 11, we are promised that the Word will come to pass for you if you will obey and practice it. There is no limit to what God's power can do. When you learn to practice it with faith there is no limit to what you can accomplish.

You can learn to command with the Magic Word, and all things will be done as you wish. Remember, you must always give thanks for the blessings you receive and give thanks in advance when you pray for the blessings you expect to receive.

Psalms 30:2: The healing power of the Magic Word is hereby demonstrated, and you can speak the Magic Word and be healed but you must obey all the laws.

Jeremiah 5:15: Many people often look far away for something that is very close to them. The Magic Word is in your mouth and heart but you must put it into action. You alone must do the work. Praise God's sacred Word and put your trust in it and have no fear of what outside things and conditions can do to you. The Word will give you patience and keep you from temptation.

Deuteronomy 5:11: Why do people swear, "By God"? They know it is a word of power and stronger than their own. Why not swear, "By Smith" or "By Jones"? To curse or condemn, why say, "God damn"? God's Word is a WORD of POWER. The meaning of this is that you must not use the sacred name to harm others and you must not use it for selfish desires, such as coveting something that belongs to another without giving proper value. You, of course, could not and would not use the name of the Lord in vain if you have love for others, and understand the law that if you harm others you harm yourself more. Wrong thinking about others is taking the sacred name in vain. To repeat: you must obey all the laws to get your reward.

Isaiah 7:14: The name Immanuel means God With Us, proving and fulfilling the law. Repeat the words "ALMIGHTY saves me." Repeating or concentrating on either of the names or words will get results.

14

The Greek form of the name Joshua, or Jeshua, a contraction of Jehoshua, that is, Help of the ALMIGHTY or God. Read Numbers 13:16.

Psalms 4:4: Throughout the Bible we find the command to keep quiet, be peaceful and still. Concentrating and repeating the Magic Word when you are in bed, quiet and still, will get greater results.

Psalms 5:3; Psalms 55:17: These are your instructions for the time to pray, or to pronounce the Magic Word, ALMIGHTY, and it is made plain that you should speak it and that the Lord will hear and answer your prayer. The Bible plainly states that there is a time for every purpose under the sun.

Psalms 69:13: There is no question but that all things must be done at the right time to get the best results, and the acceptable time for you to pray is, of course, when you need things. But if you follow God's plan and rule as outlined in the Bible for the hour and place to pray, you certainly will get better results because in this way you will be obeying the law.

Isaiah 30:7: This further proves you can get the best results by keeping quiet and sitting still. Concentrating in peace and quiet gives you power and good results.

Isaiah 30:15: You must be quiet, concentrate, meditate and silently repeat the Magic Word, ALMIGHTY, or say and repeat, ALMIGHTY HEARS AND ANSWERS MY CALL.

Lamentations 5:21: God, through the sacred word, ALMIGHTY, can renew your mind and body just as well today as he did in days of old.

We continue to find proof throughout the Bible that miracles are possible today just as they were in the past. GOD'S LAW IS ETERNAL. IT ALWAYS WAS and IT ALWAYS WILL BE. IT ALWAYS HAS WORKED AND ALWAYS WILL WORK. You have the power to put that MAGIC WORD, ALMIGHTY, into action and get results.

Chapter III

THE SACRED NAME AND WORD ALMIGHTY

What a joy it is to find just the right word for the right occasion! -- Proverbs 15:23.

The Sovereign Lord has taught me what to say, so that I can strengthen the weary. Every morning he makes me eager to hear what he is going to teach me. -- Isaiah 50:4.

YOU MUST BE DOERS OR USERS OF THE DIVINE WORD, ALMIGHTY!

The angel asked, "Why do you want to know my name? It is a name of wonder." -- Judges 13:18

Although men have spent a lifetime searching for the Magic Word of Power and many of them have failed to find it, it is made plain in the Bible just what it is.

It is not in heaven, that thou shouldest say, Who shall go up for us to heaven, and bring it unto us, that we may hear it, and do it?

Neither is it beyond the sea, that thou shouldest say, who shall go over the sea with us, and bring it unto us, that we may hear it, and do it? -- Deuteronomy 12-13.

The reason people have not found the secret word is because they have looked far away for it and the Bible says the way to find heaven is to look within. The Bible further states that it is very near, in the mind and heart. You can find it and the way to use it by reading the Bible. It was first revealed to Moses: And I appeared unto Abraham, unto Isaac, and unto Jacob, by the name of God Almighty...-- Exodus 6:3.

WORD

Do not add anything to what I command you, and do not take anything away. Obey the commands of the Lord your God that I have given you. -- Deuteronomy 4:2.

He made you go hungry, and then he gave you manna to eat, food that you and your ancestors had never eaten before. He did this to teach you that you must not depend on bread alone to sustain you, but on everything that the Lord says. -- Deuteronomy 8:3.

The Lord gave the word: great was the company of those that published it. -- Psalms 69:11.

Remember the word unto thy servant, upon which thou hast caused me to hope. -- Psalms 119:49.

What a joy it is to find just the right word for the right occasion! -- Proverbs 15:23.

The Lord hates evil thoughts, but he is pleased with friendly words. -- Proverbs 15:26.

An idea well expressed is like a design of gold, set in silver. -- Proverbs 25:11.

God keeps every promise he makes. He is like a shield for all who seek his protection.
-- Proverbs 30:5.

If you wander off the road to the right or the left, you will hear his voice behind you saying, "Here is the road. Follow it." -- Isaiah 30:21.

Yes, grass withers and flowers fade, but the word of our God endures forever. -- Isaiah 40:8.

The Sovereign Lord has taught me what to say, so that I can strengthen the weary. Every morning he makes me eager to hear what he is going to teach me. -- Isaiah 50:4.

Look up at the heavens; look at the earth! The heavens will disappear like smoke; the earth will wear out like old clothing, and all its people will die like flies. But the deliverance I bring will last forever; my victory will be final. -- Isaiah 51:16.

And I make a covenant with you: I have given you my power and my teachings to be yours forever, and from now on you are to obey me and teach your children and your descendants to obey me for all time to come. -- Isaiah 59:21.

This God—how perfect are his deeds! How dependable his words! He is like a shield for all who seek his protection. -- Psalms 18:30.

The words of the Lord are true, and all his works are dependable. -- Psalms 33:4.

I keep your law in my heart, so that I will not sin against you.

Even in my suffering I was comforted because your promise gave me life.

Your word is a lamp to guide me and a light for my path.

How certain your promise is! How I love it! -- Psalms 119:11,50,105,140.

How sweet is the taste of your instructions— sweeter even than honey!

Before sunrise I call to you for help; I place my hope in your promise.

The heart of your law is truth, and all your righteous judgments are eternal. -- Psalms 119:103,147,160.

I face your holy Temple, bow down, and praise your name because of your constant love and faithfulness, because you have shown that your name and your commands are supreme. Psalms138:2.

I wait eagerly for the Lord's help, and in his word I trust. -- Psalms 130:5.

But when I say, "I will forget the Lord and no longer speak in his name," then your message is like a fire burning deep within me. I try my best to hold it in, but can no longer keep it back. -- Jeremiah 20:9.

You spoke to me, and I listened to every word. I belong to you, Lord God Almighty, and so your words filled my heart with joy and happiness. -- Jeremiah 15:16.

I always do what God commands; I follow his will, not my own desires. -- Job 23:12.

What the wise say brings them honor, but fools are destroyed by their own words.
-- Ecclesiastes 10:12.

Think before you speak, and don't make any rash promises to God. He is in heaven and you are on earth, so don't say any more than you have to. -- Ecclesiastes 5:2.

Return to the Lord, and let this prayer be your offering to him: Forgive all our sins and accept our prayer, and we will praise you as we have promised. -- Hosea 14:2.

"Is there a limit to my power?" the Lord answered. "You will soon see whether what I have said will happen or not!" -- Numbers 11:23.

The Lord created the heavens by his command, the sun, moon, and stars by his spoken word. -- Psalms 33:6.

Do not use my name for evil purposes, for I, the Lord your God, will punish anyone who misuses my name. -- Deuteronomy 5:11.

You hear my voice in the morning; at sunrise I offer my prayer and wait for your answer.
-- Psalms 5:3.

Morning, noon, and night my complaints and groans go up to him, and he will hear my voice. -- Psalms 55:17.

But as for me, I will pray to you, Lord; answer me, God, at a time you choose. Answer me because of your great love, because you keep your promise to save. -- Psalms 69:13.

Bring us back to you, Lord! Bring us back! Restore our ancient glory. -- Lamentations 5:21

Chapter IV

WHAT THE BIBLE TEACHES

The Bible is a book of laws - physical, natural, mental, spiritual and time laws.

The Bible is simple when rightly understood. It teaches the Divine Law, its uses and abuses. Whether a law is divine or natural, it is made plain that if you disobey the law, you must pay the penalty, and if you obey or follow the law, your reward is certain.

The Bible does not teach reward after death but promises reward or a reaping now while you are here on this earth. Too many have preached that we should live a life of sacrifice here on earth and wait until after death to receive the reward. This is not what people want. They want something practical. They want to receive their reward here on earth. If they put forth the right effort, they want to know that they will receive the reward here on earth.

All natural laws teach and prove that we do get our reward on this earth. Job obeyed the law and got twice as much as he had while he was still on earth. There is nothing in the Bible saying these laws will not work today, and the Bible proves that they do.

Sowing and Reaping

When you plant or sow, you cultivate and then you reap. For instance, you plant wheat seeds, give them water and sunshine, and when the seeds come up, you cultivate them; the wheat grows and you reap wheat, not corn. This is a natural law, but it is a divine law because you cannot change it. It has always worked, and it always will work.

The same law governs your acts, thoughts and deeds. What you concentrate or think about you will reap according to the thoughts you send out. If you concentrate on money and work to get it, you will get money.

Nothing in the Bible is plainer than this. It is a natural law of cause and effect that everything brings forth after its own kind. If you think right, act right and do right, your reward is sure. If you break the commandments and the law and do evil, your punishment is sure.

Everything brings forth after its kind. The fruit you reap is exactly the same as the seed you sow. So, too, you must expect to reap from thoughts, acts and deeds exactly as you have sown.

Today I am giving you the choice between a blessing and a curse; a blessing, if you obey the commands of the Lord your God that I am giving you today; but a curse, if you disobey these commands and turn away to worship other gods that you have never worshiped before. -- Deuteronomy 11:26-28.

Again, it is made plain that a reward will come to you for every good deed, no matter how small. The divine law never fails to pay off. You will find it helpful to read over all the Bible quotations on sowing and reaping.

Power of the Word

By the Word of the Lord were the heavens made, and all the host of them by the breath of his mouth. For he spoke, and it was done; He commanded and it stood fast. -- Psalms 33: 6,9. The Bible teaches that there is power in the Word. God spoke the Word, commanding, "Let there be light" and there was light.

The Bible says that we are saved by the Word, so when you learn the Word and how to use it, you will have unlimited power.

Chapter V

HOW TO SOLVE YOUR PROBLEMS BY DIVINE LAWS

Visualize and Imagine

And he said, "Now then, these are all one people and they speak one language; this is just the beginning of what they are going to do. Soon they will be able to do anything they want! -- Genesis 11:6.

Whatever you imagine, you can do. If you cannot make a mental picture of a thing, you cannot create it. Everything that is accomplished must go through three processes.
When a great artist starts to paint a picture he must first visualize or imagine just what he intends to paint. He has to really see the perfected picture. Then he gets the material and paints the picture, which is a realization of his vision or imagination.

When an architect gets ready to draw the plans for a building he first has the picture of the building in his mind. Next, he makes the drawings for the building, and the third step is for the workers to erect the building. When this is completed the original vision or imagination becomes real.
If you can visualize or imagine, or think yourself into being sick, you can just as easily vision or imagine yourself into being perfectly well. The greater vision and imagination that anyone has, the greater success they can make of themselves. People are often called dreamers, but if you can imagine and visualize a thing you can make dreams come true. That is why it is so important to meditate and concentrate on whatever problem you wish to solve. If you cannot see yourself happy,

healthy and successful, then you cannot become happy, healthy and successful.

Read everything in the Bible under visions and imaginations and you will see the wisdom of making the mental picture of the thing you desire.

Wisdom and Power of Spirit

Joshua son of Nun was filled with wisdom, because Moses had appointed him to be his successor. The people of Israel obeyed Joshua and kept the commands that the Lord had given them through Moses. -- Deuteronomy 34.9.

Tell the priests carrying the Covenant Box that when they reach the river, they must wade in and stand near the bank. Then Joshua said to the people, Come here and listen to what the Lord your God has to say. -- Joshua 3:8-9.

I will give you a new heart and a new mind. I will take away your stubborn heart of stone and give you an obedient heart. -- Ezekiel 36:26.

Then he answered and spake unto me, saying, This is the word of the Lord unto Zerubbabel, saying, Not by might, or by power, but by my spirit, saith the Lord of hosts. -- Zechariah 4:6.

He answered, These are the four winds; they have just come from the presence of the Lord of all the earth. -- Zechariah 6:5.

He reached out what seemed to be a hand and grabbed me by the hair. Then in this vision God's spirit lifted me high in the air and took me to Jerusalem. He took me to the inner entrance of the north gate of the Temple, where there was an idol that was an outrage to God. -- Ezekiel 8:3.

Fear

Everything I fear and dread comes true. -- Job 3:25.
All around them terror is waiting; it follows them at every step. -- Job 18:11.
We have been through disaster and ruin; we live in danger and fear. -- Lamentations 3:47.

Renew the Body Through the Mind

And be renewed in the spirit of your mind;
And that ye put on the new man, which after God is created in righteousness, and true holiness.
Wherefore putting away lying, speak every man truth with his neighbor: for we are members one of another.
Bring us back to you, Lord! Bring us back! Restore our ancient glory. -- Lamentations 5:21.

Be Still and Meditate

Pause a moment, Job, and listen; consider the wonderful things God does. -- Job 37.14
Instead, they find joy in obeying the Law of the Lord, and they study it day and night.
-- Psalms 1:2.
Stop fighting," he says, "and know that I am God, supreme among the nations, supreme over the world. -- Psalms 46:10.
Tremble with fear and stop sinning; think deeply about this, when you lie in silence on your beds. -- Psalms 4:4.
Better to eat a dry crust of bread with peace of mind than have a banquet in a house full of trouble. -- Proverbs 17:1.

Think Right Thoughts

If your goals are good, you will be respected, but if you are looking for trouble, that is what you will get. -- Proverbs 11:27. People who set traps for others get caught themselves. People who start landslides get crushed. -- Proverbs 26:27.

Music or Sound Cures

So give us the order, sir, and we will look for a man who knows how to play the harp. Then when the evil spirit comes on you, the man can play his harp, and you will be all right again. -- I Samuel 16:16.

False Pride

Your pride has deceived you. Your capital is a fortress of solid rock; your home is high in the mountains, and so you say to yourself, "Who can ever pull me down?
Even though you make your home as high as an eagle's nest, so that it seems to be among the stars, yet I will pull you down. -- Obadiah 1:3-4.

Love, the Basic Law

"Love the Lord your God with all your heart, with all your soul, and with all your mind."
This is the greatest and the most important commandment. The second most important commandment is like it: "Love your neighbor as you love yourself."

Bible References on Love

Do not take revenge on others or continue to hate them, but love your neighbors as you love yourself. I am the Lord. -- Leviticus 19:18.

Love the Lord your God with all your heart, with all your soul, and with all your strength.
-- Deuteronomy 6:5.

Love the Lord, all his faithful people. The Lord protects the faithful, but punishes the proud as they deserve. -- Psalms 31:23.

The Lord loves those who hate evil; he protects the lives of his people; he rescues them from the power of the wicked. -- Psalms 97:10.

He protects everyone who loves him, but he will destroy the wicked. -- Psalms 145:20.

I love the Lord, because he hears me; he listens to my prayers. -- Psalms 116:1.

How I love you, Lord! You are my defender. -- Psalms 18:1.

How I love your law! I think about it all day long. -- Psalms 119:97.

I hate those who are not completely loyal to you, but I love your law. -- Psalms 119:113.

You are my defender and protector; I put my hope in your promise. -- Psalms 119:114.

You treat all the wicked like rubbish, and so I love your instructions. -- Psalms 119:119.

I love your commands more than gold, more than the finest gold. -- Psalms 119:127.

See how I love your instructions, Lord. Your love never changes, so save me. -- Psalms 119:159.

The heart of your law is truth, and all your righteous judgments are eternal. -- Psalms 119:160.

I hate and detest all lies, but I love your law. -- Psalms 119: 163.

I obey your teachings; I love them with all my heart. -- Psalms 119:167.

The Lord is righteous and loves good deeds; those who do them will live in his presence.
-- Psalms 11:7.
The Lord is with me, I will not be afraid; what can anyone do to me? -- Psalms 118:6.

28

The Lord corrects those he loves, as parents correct a child of whom they are proud.
-- Proverbs 3:12.
Hate stirs up trouble, but love forgives all offenses. -- Proverbs 10:12.
I appeared to them from far away. People of Israel, I have always loved you, so I continue to show you my constant love. -- Jeremiah 31:3.
I drew them to me with affection and love. I picked them up and held them to my cheek; I bent down to them and fed them. -- Hosea 11:4.
No, the Lord has told us what is good. What he requires of us is this: to do what is just, to show constant love, and to live in humble fellowship with our God. -- Micah 6:8.
The Lord your God is with you; his power gives you victory. The Lord will take delight in you, and in his love he will give you new life. He will sing and be joyful over you. -- Zephaniah 3:17.
The fasts held in the fourth, fifth, seventh, and tenth months will become festivals of joy and gladness for the people of Judah. You must love truth and peace. -- Zechariah 8:19.
"The spark of love gives more light than the universe of truth; yet truth is in love, and in order to act the truth, you must make love the truth, for remember that the handshake of friendship, or the kiss and love of an innocent child, will do more to lift a soul to the light than the strongest and wisest argument even when tightly understood.
"Beyond the boundaries of love no thought ever passed for love is where there is everywhere. Love is a prophecy of freedom, and its song of melody is heard in the rhythmic motion of the ocean.
"Each 'fowl of the air,' each fish in the sea, and every living thing that moveth upon the earth' is the manifestation of love,

for in their subsistence love has said, 'AS I CREATE SO I PROVIDE.' Thus in every conceivable thing with form or without, with harmony or with discord - there love is manifested.

"Love is the life of every plant, of every sunset, of every soul. It is the inspiration in the happy mind, and the voice that speaks to us in the time of temptation.

"Love is the foundation of all understanding, it transcends all reasoning, for it is the fulfillment of the greatest.

"Love gives faith to all things, for love believeth in its own.

"Love symbolizes the everlasting, for it is the spirit of the beginning and its wonderful radiance of color decks each sunrise and sunset.

"Love is the breeze that blows away the clouds of doubt making the landscape of the soul radiant with joy and gladness. Each heart keeps time in unison to the rhythmic harmonies of love, for each is Love in All.

"Love has thrown into the shapeless void the breath that has given life to worlds and this viral spark or the life of man, illuminates the picture that love has painted." -- Author Unknown.

When you truly love the divine lawgiver and are willing to obey His command, then you will love Him and love everyone else. When your heart is filled with love you cannot hate for love drives hate away. When you love and have knowledge of the Magic Word, ALMIGHTY, you do not doubt. When you love you are not selfish, envious or jealous.

Prayers Answered

Elijah was the same kind of person as we are. He prayed earnestly that there would be no rain, and no rain fell on the land for three and a half years.
Give yourself to the Lord; trust in him, and he will help you. -- Psalms 37:5.
God does all this again and again. -- Job 33:29.
You hear my voice in the morning; at sunrise I offer my prayer and wait for your answer.
-- Psalms 5:3.

Give and Receive Blessings

Bring the full amount of your tithes to the Temple, so that there will be plenty of food there. Put me to the test and you will see that I will open the windows of heaven and pour out on you in abundance all kinds of good things. -- Malachi 3:10.

Fear and Doubt

Most people's problems or troubles arise through fear and doubt. When fear is eliminated most of the other troubles disappear. Fear is the father of jealousy, selfishness, anger, enmity, hatred and wrong thinking. When you have no fear, most of these other evil thoughts disappear.
At the time of a problem, or any kind of trouble, your first move should be to overcome fear and doubt. You must supplant fear with faith and hope by the use of the Magic Word, ALMIGHTY. Negative thoughts must be supplanted by good thoughts. It is just as easy to think about good, pleasant things as it is to think about wrong things.
Thinking and concentrating on faith and love, and going to work by vibrating, singing or chanting the Magic Word will prepare you to solve your problems with God's help, and in the way God wants you to solve them.

Have faith and know that ALMIGHTY is a Divine Magic Word and can make you free.

Solve and dissolve your problem by the Magic Word, ALMIGHTY. God did not create fear, doubt or any evil thing. He does not bring sickness, sorrow or any trouble on you. Your troubles are the result of your own wrong thinking and doing. You have violated some of the laws; otherwise you would not have any trouble or serious problems.

Money

This is one of the problems with which many people have to contend. The need for money is often the result of spending more than your income. When you need money you should concentrate, vibrate, sing or chant the Magic Word, ALMIGHTY, and realize that there is an abundant supply of money for everyone, and that you - if you are living in obedience to the Divine Law - are entitled to what you need.

When you pray for money, have faith and believe you are going to receive it. Go to work and do something to get it. After you sound the Magic Word and ask for what you want you should then form a mental picture of the money coming into your hands.

Sickness

If you are sick yourself and want to get well you should first visualize yourself as being in perfect health and realize that good health is normal. You must feel that God did not bring illness upon you, but that he is ready and willing, through the Magic Word, to make you well. Do not talk about sickness; talk about being well and feeling well. Start acting that way, believe that you are enjoying perfect health and you will have it.

Helping Others Who Are Sick

When you have a problem of this kind you must pray for those who are sick and visualize them as being in perfect health. Sound the Magic Word, ALMIGHTY, and when you send your message for someone else, speak it orally and put the message into the air where it will reach the source of the divine supply and heal those for whom you are praying. When someone is ill, try to get them to sound the Magic Word and ask for perfect health with the faith that their prayer will be answered.

Enemies

When you are worried over enemies or opponents, the way to solve this problem is to bless them, pray for some good to come to them, and if you can, do them some favor. Love your enemies, sound the Magic Word, and pray that they may reach an understanding. Realize that it pays to do good to everyone. Enemies disappear quickly when you learn to love them. You will then find that they become your friends.

Family Troubles

This is one of the problems that most everyone has sooner or later, and they are brought on by fear, doubts, and misunderstandings. They can be solved through the Magic Word, ALMIGHTY, if you will pray earnestly for understanding yourself, sing and sound the Magic Word and ask that those of your family in trouble be given proper understanding. Then your troubles will disappear.

Buying and Selling

When you want to sell a house or buy a house you should bless the one who is going to buy from you and pray that he will be happy and well satisfied with it. Sound the Magic Word and ask that only those who will like the house or whatever you are selling will look, buy and be happy with it. When you wish to buy something, bless the seller and pray that he will have what you want and that both of you will be satisfied with the deal. Remember, wrong thoughts attract the wrong kind of people. If you use the Magic Word, ALMIGHTY, and pray, you will attract the right people.

Seeking a New Position

When you are out of employment and want to secure a new position, broadcast your message through the Magic Word, ALMIGHTY, and offer good services. Bless the party who is going to employ you and give thanks in advance for the position because if you have the right kind of faith you know you are going to get a good position. Hold the thought that you are going to be happy in the new position and that someone needs your services just as much as you need the position. The Divine Law tells us that there is always a place for those who render good services.

New Home and Changes

This is a problem often confronting people: Conditions make it necessary to sell or leave an old home and to make radical changes. If you own a beautiful home which you have loved and enjoyed, but when it becomes necessary to make a change and sell a home do so without any regrets, believing that the Divine Power will bring you a new home that you will like even better, in nearly every instance, you will acquire a home that is better than the one you just sold. Pray that the people who buy your old home will be just as happy as you were living in it. Bless the home and leave it with love, looking forward with love for the new home.

When you find it necessary to make a change, vibrate the Magic Word and pray that it is all for the best and that God's will be done, and not yours. There is nothing better than having faith and looking forward with confidence. When you have the proper faith, visualize your problem and solve it through the Magic Word, ALMIGHTY.

Worry

Worry comes through fear, doubt and lack of faith. You never solved a problem by worrying and you never will. Worry takes your energy and strength. Do everything you know to do to overcome worry. Instead of thinking the worst is going to happen, think of love, faith and all good things, and sound the Magic Word believing that you can solve your problem by a hopeful attitude with positive thoughts. It is just as easy to think positive thoughts as it is to think negative thoughts, which bring worry.

How to Produce Harmony

Harmony in mind and body is all-important and you must get in tune with the infinite power. The Magic Word, ALMIGHTY, will yield excellent results; however, there are many other words and sounds which will help different people. You can vibrate, chant, sing or hum, OH HO, AH HA, AUM OM, MOM, LOVE, LIVE, ELOHIM, JAH or DO RE MI. Any of these that will put you in tune and produce harmony are good to use.

You must get your chord or keynote and this will put your mind and body in harmony. Find the kind of music that you like, get phonograph records and listen to them. The kind of music that will soothe you and put you to sleep is the best for you. When you become quiet and feel that you can drop off to sleep, sound the Magic Word and you will get good results.

WORK

Many people do not know when they have troubles or misfortunes that if they go to work at something the problem is soon solved and the troubles disappear. You can help to solve your problem by putting the Magic Word into action while you work. Often when you work at something you do not like, or clean up a difficult job, it helps you because it relieves your mind. The mind, like the body, must be kept free and clean in order to be active and function at its best.

PRAY FOR WHAT YOU NEED

Many people do not know how to pray. They pray for things they want and not for just what they need. God knows best and will give you what you need. You may think you want something that God may think not best for you. A man once solved all his financial problems by getting his wife to agree to buy only what they needed and not everything they wanted when his salary check came in every month. The result was that he got out of debt and accumulated considerable property and had an income sufficient for all his and her needs.

He said, "My wife and I could have spent all my salary check every month for all the things we wanted but we could get along without these things. If we had spent the entire salary check for the things we desired we would never have been out of debt."

A man in Wall Street, by working hard, studying and applying the right rules, made more than a million dollars in the stock market. He thought he wanted two or three million, although he did not need the million he acquired. The result was that in trying to get more money he did not need, he lost the one million he had. Then he had to go to work starting from scratch, and found that when he bought only what he needed he could get along without the one million. If he had used the natural law and followed the Divine Law and practiced the Magic Word, ALMIGHTY, he would have found peace, happiness and contentment had he not tried to make money too fast.

HAVING YOUR OWN WAY

Many people have wrecked their lives and brought failure and misfortune upon themselves by insisting upon having their own way. This is stubbornness and should be overcome. How do you know that your way is the right way? Follow the Divine Law and do things God's way.

Two sisters inherited a home that cost over three hundred thousand dollars. The house was too large for their needs and they had no use for it, nor did they have the money to maintain a home of this size. It was too large for most any family and no one would buy it for a home. An institution offered them $125,000 for this house. They refused to sell. Later, they needed to sell badly and received an offer of $75,000, which they also refused because they had been offered $125,000 and said that they would not sell unless they got $125,000. They had decided to have it their way and to not accept a price they had been offered.

Years later, they were unable to pay the taxes, the house was sold and they were evicted, thereby losing the house because they wanted a price that suited their way. Had they prayed for Divine guidance a message would have come to them to accept $125,000 for a home they could not use nor keep up.
Many men and women have told what happened to them when they tried to have things their own way, and in later years found out their way was the wrong way, but it was too late and they suffered disappointment and misfortune. How often we hear people say, after someone has done them an injury, "I'll get even with that person if it takes me all my life."

That is having things their way and they suffer for years trying to get even when forgiveness and returning good for evil would have brought them happiness and saved a lot of trouble and anxiety.

The Divine Laws are perfect and you will make no mistake in following them. Change your mind and change your ways. Sing and sound the Magic Word, which will put your mind and body in harmony and bring you peace and happiness.

LOOKING BACKWARD

It has been said that looking backward brings nothing but regrets. If you have had misfortune and disappointment it will do you no good to dwell upon them. Do not drag your mistakes and misfortunes of the past into the future. Face the future with faith and hope. Forget the past and you will solve your problem. Remember what happened to Lot's wife. She looked back and turned into a pillar of salt. This means that she lived in the past, therefore made no progress and did not move forward more than a pillar of salt could move forward under its own power. You can't do anything about the past, but you certainly can take care of the future by making it better than the past through the use of the Magic Word and the Divine Law.

HATRED, ANGER, JEALOUSY, DOUBT AND ENMITY

All these things hinder your progress and can never do you any good. The sooner you eliminate them the sooner you will realize that you have solved your problems and that your problems will be answered. Just read in the Bible what is said about all of these things and how they mar your progress and happiness. It has been said, "Whom the gods wish to destroy they first make mad." An angry man has bad judgment; he will act wrong and act against his own best interests. The Bible says, "Let not your angry passions rise, and not let the sun go down upon your wrath." The reason for this is: Going to bed at night without forgiving someone whom you think has wronged you leaves a burden upon your mind which will prevent peaceful sleep and interfere with your progress in every way.

After you fully understand the Divine Law you will supplant hatred, anger, jealousy, doubt and enmity with love. This is the fulfilling of the law and will help you to live in harmony. You cannot expect peace and happiness, or accomplish your desires and get what you want, unless you have removed from your mind and heart all of these things that interfere with your progress. There is no use applying the Magic Word, chanting or singing it until you have a clean mind, a clean heart and a clean body.

LOVE

Look up the concordance in the Bible and read everything on love. You will learn that it is the most important thing in life. If you love your neighbor and your fellowmen you will find happiness. It is, indeed, the greatest thing on earth. It is the greatest power on earth. Men go to war and lose their lives for the love of their country. A mother will sacrifice everything she has on earth for a son because she loves him.

Why does the Bible say to love those that hate you and to return good for evil? It is because giving love for hatred is obeying the Divine Law and your reward is certain. Did anyone ever get a reward by hating someone?

When you can return good for evil you have reached the stage where you can make the divine Magic Word work, solve all your problems and accomplish all your desires. When you are in perfect harmony through the law of love, all good things will flow to you.

FORGIVENESS

The Bible makes it plain that we must forgive others if we expect forgiveness ourselves. Every night before you go to sleep you should ask forgiveness for any wrong you might have done anyone and pray for blessings on those you think have wronged you. If you can do this, love is flowing through your mind and heart and you are on the right road.

Many men and women have wrecked their lives became they could not forgive and forget. How much better it is to forgive quickly and bless the other person, even if he should be wrong! It brings freedom and happiness to you.

CONFESSION

The Bible makes it strong that you should confess your sins and errors. You will make greater progress if you confess orally. If you have no one to whom you can talk, go into the open, in a quiet place, speak in a quiet voice and confess your mistakes. Get them out of your system. Another good way is to write on paper all the mistakes you have made or anything that is troubling you. Burn the paper and you are free. After this repeat the Magic Word and make your prayers. You will sleep better, have better health and find that your problems soon will be solved.

SHORT CIRCUIT IN MIND AND BODY

How often have you pressed a button to turn on an electric light and found that the light did not come on? If, on examination, you found the circuit was on then you knew there was a short circuit leading to the light bulb. When this short circuit was removed the light came on. This is what happens to your mind when you are thinking wrong thoughts, such as, hatred, anger, jealousy, doubt and enmity. This produces a short circuit in your mind which affects the body and you will not be well, happy, or successful until you remove the short circuit. This you can do by right thinking and supplanting the other evil thoughts with love and good thoughts. By putting good thoughts into action and doing something good for someone else you put your own mind and body in harmony and the short circuit disappears. By singing, chanting and humming the Magic Word, ALMIGHTY, you can produce harmony in mind and body.

CONFUSION AND CONCENTRATION

The Bible has much to say about confusion. No one can concentrate and meditate and get good results when the mind is confused. You cannot think about two things at the same time, nor can you do two things successfully at the same time. If you are thinking about some misfortune, or some wrong someone has done you, you cannot meditate or concentrate and get yourself in harmony with the perfect Divine Law. The way to overcome confusion is to get quiet and still, and repeat the Magic Word, ALMIGHTY, until there is no confusion, then whatever was disturbing your mind will have disappeared.

MEDITATION AND MENTAL PICTURE

You should always meditate quietly and alone, where there are no distractions. Think about what you want and what you need. Ask for ideas and for guidance.

Try to see a realization or a picture of what you have asked for, and see the fulfillment of what you pray for. Suppose you need money and you have prayed for money, you bless the money that is coming and give thanks for it in advance. Picture the money as being already in your hands and bless it. When you spend money or give it away, give your blessings with it. If you do not give willingly, and with a blessing that the money will be of benefit to the receiver, it is better that you do not give it. When you are going to give something to someone do not say, "I will do this, but I cannot afford it." When you give, give freely and willingly. Than say, "I know that the Divine supply is unlimited and what I need will come to me in due time."

41

THANKSGIVING AND GIVING

Following the example set by our Fathers we daily give thanks to Almighty God for his blessings. This is wonderful and as it should be. We will all be better off and happier if we give thanks every day for what we have received and for what we are about to receive. The more often we give thanks and send out blessings the more good things will return to us. When you are despondent and think you have a lot of troubles and misfortunes, sit down and write out all the blessings you have received throughout life. They will so far overbalance your seeming troubles and misfortunes that you will feel like giving thanks instead of feeling sorry for yourself, and lamenting your condition. Many so-called misfortunes are blessings in disguise. I have had this proven many times in my life.

GIVING THANKS

The Bible teaches us to give thanks day and night. You should give thanks for everything you have received, bless everyone who has helped you and when you pray for anything give thanks in advance. Say, "Lord, the Divine Power, I am thankful because I know my prayer is going to be answered." This is showing your faith and then if you act and work in accordance with the Divine Law your prayer will be answered. Read everything in the Bible under praise and giving thanks and you will learn how important it is. No matter how small a favor someone may do for you, show your appreciation by thanking them. You will feel better and they will feel better. Some people say, I have paid so and so for what he did for me; I do not owe him any thanks. By refusing to give thanks to the other person and blessing him he was hurting himself and putting off the good that might come to him.

God works in mysterious ways his wonders to perform. It may take a little time for us to see why things that have happened are for the best. Giving to others, or to charity of any kind, is a problem which each individual must solve for himself. The

Bible says that 10 per cent of your income is about the right amount. You certainly owe something to the Lord and his cause after you have received benefit. You should always try to help those who are trying to help themselves. Give to people who are in need and not to people who are just asking for something because they want it. Do not give to beggars because you are encouraging them to continue to try to get something for nothing. A man once asked Andrew Carnegie to give him 25¢ because he was hungry. Carnegie answered, "I have never paid a man to beg, but if you really want to work for money, I will give you a job." The man went to work for Carnegie and made a great success of himself.

Many people have the wrong idea about how or where to find God. The Divine Power is always within you and in the air you breathe. The Magic Word, ALMIGHTY, is always with you to help you at any time or any place. God can help you whether you are on the water or under the water, in a submarine. He can reach you in a tunnel under the earth. He can reach you when you are five miles above the earth in an aeroplane, and he can answer your prayers no matter where you are, or in any and all conditions. If God could not do this he would not be God and His power would not be everlasting and divine. Some people have the idea that the only place they can find God is within the church. This is wrong. God can and will hear and answer your prayers no matter where you are. There is no limit to Divine Power, and no time or place that it will not work for you, so long as you are in harmony and are obeying the Divine Law. You are a child of God; you are born in the image and likeness of your maker and are entitled to everything you need through obedience to the Divine Law. All you need to learn is how to work and put the Divine Magic Word, ALMIGHTY, into action, and your prayers will be answered.

Chapter VI

WORLD PROBLEMS

For thousands of years nations have gone to war and in many instances war has been started just because some ruler was greedy for power and brought on a war in the hopes of increasing his power. This ruler never thought of the loss of life or the property of others. It is a well known fact that after political leaders, kings and dictators get their countries in bad shape financially by making mistakes and wasting the people's money, they start a war and then try to blame all the misfortunes of the people on the war. The facts are, they made the mistakes before the war and they had started the war to cover up their mistakes. In most instances wars are not started to protect the rights of the people; they are started by one nation wanting to get something for nothing and trying to gain control of the business and commercial interests of the world, the aim of that nation being to gain world domination. England started wars to obtain more territory and at one time she controlled practically all the trade of the world. Every war Germany has fought has been to further her trade interests and to seek domination. Hitler didn't start a war with Poland because Poland had done something he didn't like. He started the war to acquire Poland and other countries and to dominate the commercial business of the world. If this had not been the case, when he succeeded in defeating Poland, he would have quit. In fact, he said he was going to quit after he took a certain amount of land from Poland. If Hitler had succeeded in defeating Russia he would have then crossed the channel to defeat England and, if he had succeeded there, he would then have tackled the United States, and, if successful, he would have attacked his ally Japan because his whole objective was to dominate the business of the world. Rulers always find something to fight about when they decide they need the business of another country. Wars never solved a problem. If they did, wars would not continue to be fought every twenty or thirty years. Nothing has ever been gained by war. The winner loses because the cost of material, men and money is greater than any possible benefits. If the money that has been spent on wars during the past two hundred years had been used for constructive purposes no country would be paying taxes to amount to anything, every desert would blossom like a rose and the trillions of dollars that have been used for wars could be used for research to overcome all diseases. People would be happier, healthier and contented in a land of plenty, and poverty would be unknown.

If every nation on the face of the earth worked as hard and prepared to maintain peace, as it does to prepare for war, there would be no war. If the rulers of all the countries of the world believed in God's Divine Law and were willing to follow the Golden Rule, all problems could be settled without resorting to war.

As soon as World War II ended, in 1945, the United States started spending billions of dollars getting ready for another war. If we went into this last war to bring an end to wars, and to make the world safe for democracy, why do we have to start to get ready for another war? This is proof that wars do not settle any problems.

The United States has never gone to war with the objective of gaining territory, and if we do not want territory or anything from other countries, why enter war? Why should we develop the atomic bomb and the hydrogen bomb to fight Russia? Our country is making it plain that we are preparing to fight Russia. Can anyone blame Russia for getting ready to fight a country that is preparing to fight her? Politicians and political leaders, in order to hold their own jobs which are the most important things to them, scare the taxpayers into letting them be taxed for money to start another war. They rule the people through fear. If they ruled through love and understanding there would be no war. This is the only way the United States and the rest of the world can solve the problem and bring about world peace. We have got to stop talking of

45

war and preparing for war. We must work for peace, pray for peace and follow the Divine command: Love thy neighbour as thyself. Love those who hate us and try to help instead of fight them. With the advance in science and modern weapons of war the world cannot stand a third World War. Civilization will be wiped out. The smartest men we have know this to be a fact. The people must be aroused and made to realize that they must not support and follow political leaders whose aim is to lead our whole country into war in order to hold their own jobs. The taxpayer should be willing to be taxed for money to be used to bring about universal peace, but not for taxes to start another war, which, if we could win, would not solve the problem. If the people were allowed to vote on war there would be no war. If women were allowed to vote to decide whether or not there would be another war, they would not vote to send their sons to be slaughtered. The Divine Law of love must be followed sooner or later. The United States should take the lead in starting the move for universal peace, and let the world know it does not want to fight and that war can never permanently settle any problem. If we do this, then we can look forward to a better world and universal peace.

Chapter VII

BROADCAST YOUR PRAYERS

Radio and Wireless Forecast in the Bible:

Curse not the king, no, not in thy thought:

and curse not the rich in thy bedchamber: for
a bird of the air shall carry the ,voice, and that ,
which hath wings shall tell the matter. -- Ecclesiastes 10:20
.

The bird of the air referred to in this verse is the aeroplane,
equipped with radio, flying through the air without wires or
any connection except the sound waves and, equipped to send
radio messages, can direct its message anywhere, to other
planes flying in the air, to radio stations or to ships at sea.
This was one of the greatest inventions of the world -- wireless
and radio -- and it has proved be of more benefit to mankind
than any other invention.

HOW DOES THE RADIO WORK WITHOUT WIRES AND CARRY MESSAGES IN EVERY DIRECTION?

Radio works as the result of sound waves which once set in motion continue to move and can be picked up by a radio receiving set tuned into the same wave length. You cannot see these sound waves, but you know they work. Man no longer needs wires to transmit messages. You can tune in on different stations of different wavelengths. You can tune off, or tune out stations that you do not want. Before wireless and radio were invented sound waves had been discovered and many men knew something about how they traveled, but they had not learned how to record and receive sound waves until they discovered radio. More proof of what the Bible says, that whatever a man imagines, he can do. The man who invented wireless and radio imagined he could do it, and he did it. This is the greatest proof of the unseen forces being the most powerful. You cannot see the airwaves or sound waves, but you can hear them and you know they work. You cannot see the Divine force that is in the air, but it is there and all-powerful, and will work miracles for you if you will have faith and put it into action.

PUT YOUR MESSAGE IN THE AIR

If you speak into the air, and speak the Magic Word ALMIGHTY, you are broadcasting your prayers and desires when you say, "I am love," or make your demands to God, speaking the word through the air. You will get greater results when you sound the Magic Word. It will start the wave of happiness and prosperity and good health moving toward you. And, what you send out when you speak the word into the air will return to you. Remember, fear and doubt are the only things which can cause a short circuit in your mind and body, and prevent all good things from flowing to you. You must supplant fear with faith, and hope is held out with love and the Magic Word, and Divine power of the Magic Word ALMIGHTY, that you will receive what you ask for and find happiness in Heaven and here on earth.

The Bible is simple and plain, yet to people who do not understand it in the right way it is complicated and mysterious. It is simple and easy if you read it correctly and accept it for what it means.

FROM WHERE DOES DIVINE POWER COME?

It is neither separate nor apart from you, but it is in you and a part of you. The Divine power is what most people call God. It is everywhere, just like the air is everywhere. You cannot live without air, and you cannot live without the Divine power, which created life. Then you can say, "God is in the air." That is right. Air is the most important thing, for when God breathed air into Adam, he became a living being. You breathe the power of the Magic Word, "ALMIGHTY," when you sound the word, and breathing in air, taking deep breaths, gives you Divine power. Then does this not prove why the Bible says you cannot see God, and that no one has ever seen Him? You cannot see the air, but you can feel it, and you know it has great power for construction or destruction, depending upon how you use it. The eye is deceptive, therefore, when we reason from the objective of what we see, we are often wrong. The magician proves that the hand is quicker than the eye, and we believe what the eye sees, but it is often wrong. You can prove this to yourself. Look down a railroad track until you see the two rails come together. Your eye perceives that this is true and that the railroad rails do come together, but it is an optical illusion. They do not come together.

Follow your still small voice, or the overseeing eye, the inner eye, which is in contact with the Divine power. It is always right. A woman's intuition is always right and she can depend upon it, but when she reasons from the objective she is wrong. We should all listen to the message from the Divine power and follow it.

WHY DO YOU WANT TO GO TO HEAVEN?

The reason people want to go to Heaven is to find peace, quiet and happiness which they have not found on this earth due to their own fault and failure to understand the Divine power in the sacred name and Magic Word. Let me make it plain to you. If you cannot find happiness and contentment on this earth, you will not find it in the world to come as the Bible teaches that you reap just what you sow and the heaven you go to will be according to your deeds done on this earth.

Others cannot show you the way to heaven on earth, nor can they find it for you. You have to do that for yourself. One may be able to show you the right road and the way to find happiness, but you must have the faith and do the work yourself. The trouble with most people is they expect others to do the work for them. The Divine word, the Magic Word, ALMIGHTY, never promised that. You must learn the truth, and practice its teachings. Work with the Word. Sound and speak the Magic Word, ALMIGHTY, which is the way to call the Divine power from the air and get the answers to your prayers. The Bible tells you the plain truth and you must accept it on faith, believe it and then prove to yourself by obedience to the law and to the Magic Word, ALMIGHTY.

Chapter VIII

SOUND, SONG AND SINGING

God goes up to his throne. There are shouts of joy and the blast of trumpets, as the Lord goes up. -- Psalms 47:5.

How happy are the people who worship you with songs, who live in the light of your kindness! -- Psalms 89:15.

You like to compose songs, as David did, and play them on harps. -- Amos 6:5.

Lord, look upon us from heaven, where you live in your holiness and glory. Where is your great concern for us? Where is your power? Where are your love and compassion? Do not ignore us. -- Isaiah 63:15.

Sing praise to the Lord, who rules in Zion! Tell every nation what he has done! -- Psalms 9:11.

I will sing to you, O Lord, because you have been good to me. -- Psalms 13-6.

So I will triumph over my enemies around me. With shouts of joy I will offer sacrifices in his Temple; I will sing, I will praise the Lord. -- Psalms 27:6.

Sing praise to the Lord, all his faithful people! Remember what the Holy One has done, and give him thanks!

So I will not be silent; I will sing praise to you. Lord, you are my God; I will give you thanks forever. -- Psalms 30:4,12.

You are my hiding place; you will save me from trouble. I sing aloud of your salvation, because you protect me. -- Psalms 32:7.

Sing a new song to him, play the harp with skill, and shout for joy! -- Psalms 33:3.

He taught me to sing a new song, a song of praise to our God. Many who see this will take warning and will put their trust in the Lord. -- Psalms 40:3.

Yet the Lord will command his loving kindness in the daytime, and in the night his song shall be with me, and my prayer unto the God of my life. -- Psalms 42:8.

Sing praises to God, sing praises: sing praises unto our King, sing praises.

For God is the King of all the earth: sing ye praises with understanding. -- Psalms 47:6,7.

But I will sing of thy power; yea, I will sing aloud of thy mercy in the morning: for thou hast been my defense and refuge in the day of my trouble. -- Psalms 59:16.

Sing unto God, ye kingdoms of the earth; O sing praises unto the Lord; Selah. -- Psalms 68:32.

But I will declare forever; I will sing praises to the God of Jacob. -- Psalms 75:9.

I spend the night in deep thought; I meditate, and this is what I ask myself. -- Psalms 77:6.

Sing aloud unto God our strength: make a joyful noise unto the God of Jacob. -- Psalms 81:1.

It is a good thing to give thanks unto the Lord, and to sing praises unto thy name, O most High. -- Psalms 92:1.

O come, let us sing unto the Lord: let us make a joyful noise to the rock of our salvation.
-- Psalms 95:1.

O sing unto the Lord a new song: sing unto the Lord, all the earth.

Sing unto the Lord, bless his name; shew forth his salvation from day to day. -- Psalms 96:1-2.

O sing unto the Lord a new song; for he hath done marvelous things: his right hand, and his holy arm, hath gotten him the victory. -- Psalms 98:1.

I will sing of mercy and judgment: unto thee, O Lord, will I sing. -- Psalms 101:1.

I will sing unto the Lord as long as I live: I will sing praise to my God while I have my being.
-- Psalms 104:33.

The Lord is my strength and song, and is become my salvation. -- Psalms 118:14.

Thy statutes have been my songs in the house of my pilgrimage. -- Psalms 119:54.

Praise the Lord; for the Lord is good: sing praises unto his name; for it is pleasant. -- Psalms 135:3.

For there they that carried us away captive required of us a song; and they that wasted us required of us mirth, saying, Sing us one of the songs of Zion. -- Psalms 137:3.

I will sing a new song unto thee, O God: upon a psaltery and an instrument of ten strings will I sing praises unto thee. -- Psalms 144:9.

They shall abundantly utter the memory of thy great goodness, and shall sing of thy righteousness. -- Psalms 145:7.

While I live will I praise the Lord: I will sing praises unto my God while I have any being. -- Psalms 146:2.

Praise ye the Lord: for it is good to sing praises unto our God; for it is pleasant; and praise is comely. -- Psalms 147:1.

Praise ye the Lord. Sing unto the Lord a new song, and his praise in the congregation of saints.

Let them praise his name in the dance: let them sing praises unto him with the tumbrel and harp. -- Psalms 149:1, 3.

Sing to the Lord because of the great things he has done. Let the whole world hear the news. -- Isaiah 12:5.

But you, God's people, will be happy and sing as you do on the night of a sacred festival. You will be as happy as those who walk to the music of flutes on their way to the Temple of the Lord, the defender of Israel. -- Isaiah 30:29.

Sing a new song to the Lord; sing his praise, all the world! Praise him, you that sail the sea; praise him, all creatures of the sea! Sing, distant lands and all who live there! -- Isaiah 42:10.

Break into shouts of joy, you ruins of Jerusalem! The Lord will rescue his city and comfort his people. -- Isaiah 52:9.

The Lord says to Jerusalem, "Foreigners will rebuild your walls, And their kings will serve you. In my anger I punished you, But now I will show you my favor and mercy. -- Isaiah 60:10.

Then Moses and the Israelites sang this song to the Lord: I will sing to the Lord, because he has won a glorious victory; he has thrown the horses and their riders into the sea.

The Lord is my strong defender; he is the one who has saved me. He is my God, and I will praise him, my father's God, and I will sing about his greatness. -- Exodus 15:1-2.

Miriam sang for them: "Sing to the Lord, because he has won a glorious victory; he has thrown the horses and their riders into the sea. -- Exodus 15:21.

At that time the people of Israel sang this song: "Wells, produce your water; And we will greet it with a song — Numbers 21:17.

Chapter IX

FASTING

Then all the people of Israel went up to Bethel and mourned. They sat there in the Lord's presence and did not eat until evening. They offered fellowship sacrifices and burned some sacrifices whole—all in the presence of the Lord. -- Judges 20:26.

Then they took the bones and buried them under the tamarisk tree in town, and fasted for seven days. -- I Samuel 31:13.

They grieved and mourned and fasted until evening for Saul and Jonathan and for Israel, the people of the Lord, because so many had been killed in battle. -- II Samuel 1:12.

David prayed to God that the child would get well. He refused to eat anything, and every night he went into his room and spent the night lying on the floor. -- II Samuel 12:16.

"We don't understand this," his officials said to him. "While the child was alive, you wept for him and would not eat; but as soon as he died, you got up and ate!" -- II Samuel 12:21.

The letters said: "Proclaim a day of fasting, call the people together, and give Naboth the place of honor:

They proclaimed a day of fasting, called the people together, and gave Naboth the place of honor.

When Elijah finished speaking, Ahab tore his clothes, took them off, and put on sackcloth. He refused food, slept in the sackcloth, and went about gloomy and depressed. -- I Kings 21:9,12,27.

The bravest men went and got the bodies of Saul and his sons and took them to Jabesh. They buried them there under an oak and fasted for seven days. -- I Chronicles 10:12.

So we fasted and prayed for God to protect us, and he answered our prayers. -- Ezra 8:21,23.

On the twenty-fourth day of the same month the people of Israel gathered to fast in order to show sorrow for their sins. They had already separated themselves from all foreigners. They wore sackcloth and put dust on their heads as signs of grief. Then they stood and began to confess the sins that they and their ancestors had committed. -- Nehemiah 9:1.

Throughout all the provinces, wherever the king's proclamation was made known, there was loud mourning among the Jews. They fasted, wept, wailed, and most of them put on sackcloth and lay in ashes. -- Esther 4:3.

And directed them and their descendants to observe the days of Purim at the proper time, just as they had adopted rules for the observance of fasts and times of mourning. This was commanded by both Mordecai and Queen Esther. -- Esther 9:31.
Go and get all the Jews in Susa together; hold a fast and pray for me. Don't eat or drink anything for three days and nights. My servant women and I will be doing the same. After that, I will go to the king, even though it is against the law. If I must die for doing it, I will die. -- Esther 4:16.

But when they were sick, I dressed in mourning; I deprived myself of food; I prayed with my head bowed low. -- Psalms 35:13.

I humble myself by fasting, and people insult me. -- Psalms 69:10.

My knees are weak from lack of food; I am nothing but skin and bones. -- Psalms 109:24.

The people ask, "Why should we fast if the Lord never notices? Why should we go without food if he pays no attention?" The Lord says to them, "The truth is that at the same time you fast, you pursue your own interests and oppress your workers.

Your fasting makes you violent, and you quarrel and fight. Do you think this kind of fasting will make me listen to your prayers?

When you fast, you make yourselves suffer; you bow your heads low like a blade of grass and spread out sackcloth and ashes to lie on. Is that what you call fasting? Do you think I will be pleased with that?

The kind of fasting I want is this: Remove the chains of oppression and the yoke of injustice, and let the oppressed go free. -- Isaiah 58:3,4,5,6.

In the ninth month of the fifth year that Jehoiakim was king of Judah, the people fasted to gain the Lord's favor. The fast was kept by all who lived in Jerusalem and by all who came there from the towns of Judah. -- Jeremiah 36:9.

Then the king returned to the palace and spent a sleepless night, without food or any form of entertainment. -- Daniel 6:18.

And I prayed earnestly to the Lord God, pleading with him, fasting, wearing sackcloth, and sitting in ashes. -- Daniel 9:3.
Give orders for a fast; call an assembly! Gather the leaders and all the people of Judah into the Temple of the Lord your God and cry out to him! -- Joel 1:14.

"But even now," says the Lord, "repent sincerely and return to me with fasting and weeping and mourning."

The people of Nineveh believed God's message. So they decided that everyone should fast, and all the people, from the greatest to the least, put on sackcloth to show that they had repented. -- Jonah 3:5.

The fasts held in the fourth, fifth, seventh, and tenth months will become festivals of joy and gladness for the people of Judah. You must love truth and peace. -- Zechariah 8:19.

Chapter X

HEALING

Your Most Valuable Possession

Most people, if asked what is their most valuable possession, would answer, money. That is wrong. Your most valuable possession is TIME. You exchange time for money or something that you need. Your next valuable possession is good health. Therefore, you should spend some of your time to keep in good health.

Solomon was credited with being the wisest man who ever lived. He placed knowledge and understanding above all else. If you use your time in getting knowledge you are putting it to the best advantage. Money always comes through knowledge. You cannot put knowledge to work without good health. Many people have deformities, but they overcome these and are able to make a living because they have learned how to do something despite their infirmities. If you apply the Magic Word, ALMIGHTY, to all of your problems, you will have good health, acquire knowledge and accumulate money.

We often learn through adversity. People seldom learn when they are prosperous. Nature often teaches a lesson in the value of good health by putting you flat on your back in bed, and it is after suffering an illness that you learn to take care of your health. Misfortunes and adversities often prove a blessing in disguise. We must learn by past mistakes and not repeat them in the future. Use the Magic Word and pray for the power to overcome mistakes, and you will succeed.

The Importance of Correct Deep Breathing

Since air is the most important element that keeps us alive, correct deep breathing is essential to good health. You can take breathing exercises anywhere and at any time, but you will get the best results by doing breathing exercises in bed after you are relaxed and quiet.

Twelve Breaths

Every part of your body can be stimulated and helped through correct deep breathing. The Hindus used three breaths and seven breaths, or breathing three times, resting then repeating three times, making nine breaths over three consecutive periods.

Twelve breaths are the most valuable because there are twelve organs of the body each of which need stimulation and building up through proper breathing and upon which you should concentrate while taking these breaths, and they are:

1. The *head* in which are your eyes, ears and nose. Concentrate on these organs while inhaling and exhaling your first breath for stimulation of the head and brain, which is the most important part of the body in acquiring knowledge, good health and all other things.

2. The *throat and other organs of respiration.* This breath should be to stimulate them.

3. The *lungs.* This breath is the most important as it was used by the Hindus to stimulate the lungs, the shoulders and the arms.

4. The *stomach*. The fourth breath is to stimulate the stomach and aid it in digesting the food properly.

5. The *heart*. When you practice this breath concentrate on strengthening the heart and resting it; also concentrate on very deep breathing to affect your whole circulatory system as it is through the proper functioning of the heart that good circulation and distribution of the blood depends.

6. The *bowels*. Concentrate upon keeping your bowels strong, making them active in order to eliminate poisons from your body.

7. *The back* and loins. Beginning with the 6th breath, think about the solar plexus. When the solar plexus is aroused and functions properly it feeds the nerves leading to all other parts of the body, as it is a large group of nerves serving as your receiving station for the body. This should operate smoothly because if there be a short circuit here it impedes tuning in on the Divine Power to heal your mind and body, or to ask for all your needs.

8. The *genital* organs. Breath to keep these organs strong for recreation or building up of the body. The sex forces are not to be wasted in excesses but are to be retained to build a strong healthy body.

9. The *hips* and thighs. The 9th breath should be concentrated on these.

10. The *knees*. By this time you should be breathing very deeply and try to imagine you are drawing your breath to the knees. Strong knees enable one to walk—the most popular form of exercise.

11. The *calves of the legs,* and the leg extending between the knees and ankles, must be well preserved to prevent hardening of the arteries.

12. The *feet*. The nerve centers terminate in the soles of the feet where the blood reaches the greatest extreme and begins its flow back to the heart.

Few people realize how important it is to exercise the feet and bathe them frequently. If you will read everything in the Bible under feet you will find out how vital it is to take proper care of them. Every pore of your skin is used for breathing purposes and the soles of the feet have a maximum of pores through which your skin breathes. For this reason you should take off your shoes as often as possible and let your feet get plenty of fresh air, but it is most important to keep them clean.

Sunbaths for Health

The Bible tells us that God created the sun to give light by day, and the moon to give light by night. The ancients worshipped the sun and built pyramids and monuments to the sun and the moon. They believed the sun to be God and the giver of life.

The sun gives life to plants, animals and human beings. Nothing can live without it. When heat leaves the body, the body is dead and no longer active. Compare this to the electric streetcar, which moves as long as the electric current is on but when the current is cut off, the streetcar stops and does not move until the current is again turned on.

Vegetation needs three things to produce growth and they are:

1. Sun
2. Water
3. Earth

The sun or heat is the most important because even though you do plant seeds and water them they will not germinate without heat, which is supplied by the sun.

By taking nude sunbaths in the open air your skin is stimulated as it absorbs the life-giving elements from the sun to build up a strong body. Electric heat and various electrically operated lamps can help your body and your skin, but these artificial means cannot compare with the health-giving rays of the sun on the human body. Sunbaths on the seashore where you breathe the salt air are very beneficial. Nude sunbaths always help because all of the pores of the skin are exposed allowing all the pores to breathe. Deep breathing exercises taken in the open air and in the sunshine will give you greater benefit.

References for Healing

He said, "If you will obey me completely by doing what I consider right and by keeping my commands, I will not punish you with any of the diseases that I brought on the Egyptians. I am the Lord, the one who heals you. -- Exodus 15:26.

So Moses cried out to the Lord, "O God, heal her!" -- Numbers 12:13.

"I, and I alone, am God; no other god is real. I kill and I give life, I wound and I heal, and no one can oppose what I do. -- Deuteronomy 32:39.

The Lord answered Hezekiah's prayer; he forgave the people and did not harm them.
-- II Chronicles 30:20.

I am worn out, O Lord; have pity on me! Give me strength; I am completely exhausted.
-- Psalms 6:2.

I said, "I have sinned against you, Lord; be merciful to me and heal me." -- Psalms 41:4.

Why am I so sad? Why am I so troubled? I will put my hope in God, and once again I will praise him, my savior and my God. -- Psalms 43:5.

You have made the land tremble, and you have cut it open; now heal its wounds, because it is falling apart. -- Psalms 60:2.

So that the whole world may know your will; so that all nations may know your salvation. -- Psalms 67:2.

He forgives all my sins and heals all my diseases. -- Psalms 103:3.

He healed them with his command and saved them from the grave. -- Psalms 107:20.

He heals the broken-hearted and bandages their wounds. -- Psalms 147:3.

Re: Solar Plexus

If you do, it will be like good medicine, healing your wounds and easing your pains.
-- Proverbs 3:8.

Thoughtless words can wound as deeply as any sword, but wisely spoken words can heal.
-- Proverbs 12:18.

Then he said to me, "Make the minds of these people dull, their ears deaf, and their eyes blind, so that they cannot see or hear or understand. If they did, they might turn to me and be healed." -- Isaiah 6:10.

The moon will be as bright as the sun, and the sun will be seven times brighter than usual, like the light of seven days in one. This will all happen when the Lord bandages and heals the wounds he has given his people. -- Isaiah 30:26.

But because of our sins he was wounded, beaten because of the evil we did. We are healed by the punishment he suffered, made whole by the blows he received. -- Isaiah 53:5.

Return, all of you who have turned away from the Lord; he will heal you and make you faithful. You say, "Yes, we are coming to the Lord because he is our God." -- Jeremiah 3:22.

They act as if my people's wounds were only scratches. "All is well," they say, when all is not well. -- Jeremiah 8:11.

We hoped for peace and a time of healing, but it was no use; terror came instead
-- Jeremiah 8:15.

Why do I keep on suffering? Why are my wounds incurable? Why won't they heal? Do you intend to disappoint me like a stream that goes dry in the summer? -- Jeremiah 15:18.

There is no one to take care of you, no remedy for your sores, no hope of healing for you.
-- Jeremiah 30:13.

I will make you well again; I will heal your wounds, though your enemies say, "Zion is an outcast; no one cares about her." I, the Lord, have spoken. -- Jeremiah 30:17.

The people say, Let's return to the Lord! He has hurt us, but he will be sure to heal us; he has wounded us, but he will bandage our wounds, won't he? -- Hosea 6:1.

The Lord says, I will bring my people back to me. I will love them with all my heart; no longer am I angry with them. -- Hosea 14:4.

Chapter XI

PRAY AND PRAYER

Your prayers are answered through speaking, chanting or humming and vibrating the Magic Word, ALMIGHTY. You get an answer to your prayers through meditation and concentration, which should be done in a quiet, peaceful place. Your prayers are answered by positive thoughts and words, and not by negative thoughts and acts.

When you want good health, talk about good health and think about good health. Remember, your own thoughts and words return to you. You do not want to be sick; why talk about sickness?

There are people who constantly talk about their illnesses and troubles, and in so doing they are keeping their mind on them. The way to get good health is to be positive; think and talk of good health; have only good thoughts and speak good words of everyone. When you pray and use the Magic Word you certainly would not pray for illness, you would pray for good health. Why not, when you do feel a little ill, pray for what you want, which is good health. Follow Coué's rule and say, "Every day and in every way I am getting better and better." Look in the mirror every day and say I am looking better, feeling better and looking better. Keep this up and you will soon see the results.

When you pray and sound the Magic Word, ALMIGHTY, ask for what you want and need. Do not think or talk about what you don't want. The Bible says: As a man thinketh in his heart so is he. It has also been well said that what a man loves he will become, God if he loves God, and dust if he loves dust.

If you do not want others to criticize and find fault with you, do not criticize others and find fault with them. Your own thoughts and words will return to you.

If you want love you must give love, think of love and talk of love. You cannot get love through hating and by thinking of hating people. Think positive and not negative thoughts.

When you want money concentrate on money. Do not talk about poverty or think about poverty. Never say, I am poor. This is inviting misfortune upon yourself. Make a positive statement by saying, I am rich in God's love and through the power of the Divine Magic Word I shall be rich in money. The Divine Power is unlimited, and money and everything I need will flow to me.

Holding a Grudge

This is one of the worst things anyone can do. It poisons the mind and body, creates a short circuit, and your prayers cannot be answered as long as you hold a grudge. That is why the Bible tells you to return good for evil. The idea of trying to get even with someone because they have done you a seeming injury is the worst thing you can do. The only way you can get even and get a return for yourself is to do some good for someone. Then your reward is sure. The Bible says to transform your body through the renewing of your mind. Your mind is renewed when you cleanse it of all evil thoughts and give and forgive. Your prayers will then be answered.

When you fall asleep at night repeat the Magic Word, ALMIGHTY, and say: The Divine Word is doing its work while I sleep; my mind and body is being made perfect. Plenty of sleep and rest is essential to good health, happiness and prosperity.

While you sleep the Divine Power is opening your mind to unlimited supplies of everything you need and if you concentrate it will come to you and your prayer will be answered.

Just before you fall asleep, say: The Power of the Magic Word, ALMIGHTY, will show me what to do and how to get everything I need. Then repeat: The Magic Word, ALMIGHTY, saves and protects me now. I am healed by the Magic Word, ALMIGHTY.

The Magic Word, ALMIGHTY, Works Wonders

After you have put the Magic Word to the test and proved it, as thousands of others have, you will know that it does work wonders.

When you sound the Magic Word, ALMIGHTY, into the air and ask for what you need, the sound waves carry your message throughout the world. The unseen powerful forces you are in tune with carry your message and it is received by other minds which are in tune with yours. This opens the way for you through faith to get all you need and to get an answer to your prayers. You must pray when you have any difficult problem that you will receive a message on how to work and what to do to get an answer to your prayers.

You should repeat: God created everything through the spoken word ALMIGHTY; I can do the same. The Magic Word is just as powerful today as it was when God used it in creating everything.

The Magic Word, ALMIGHTY, is God and the expression of His power. That power never becomes weak because God is eternal and everlasting. If the word had the power to work one time it has it now because God has made it plain that it is everlasting and that it does not change. Your prayers will be answered when you live in obedience to the Divine Law.

References for Praying and Prayer

Then Samuel called for all the Israelites to meet at Mizpah, telling them, "I will pray to the Lord for you there. -- I Samuel 7:5.

And they said to Samuel, "Please, sir, pray to the Lord your God for us, so that we won't die. We now realize that, besides all our other sins, we have sinned by asking for a king. -- I Samuel 12:19.

Lord Almighty, God of Israel! I have the courage to pray this prayer to you, because you have revealed all this to me, your servant, and have told me that you will make my descendants kings. -- II Samuel 7:27.

Lord my God, I am your servant. Listen to my prayer, and grant the requests I make to you today:

Listen to their prayers. If any of your people Israel, out of heartfelt sorrow, stretch out their hands in prayer toward this Temple:

Listen to their prayers. Hear them in heaven and give them victory. -- I Kings 8:28,38,45.

The priests and the Levites asked the Lord's blessing on the people. In his home in heaven God heard their prayers and accepted them. -- II Chronicles 30:27.

Look at me, Lord, and hear my prayer, as I pray day and night for your servants, the people of Israel. I confess that we, the people of Israel, have sinned. My ancestors and I have sinned. -- Nehemiah 1:6.

But we prayed to our God and kept men on guard against them day and night. -- Nehemiah 4:9.

But I am not guilty of any violence, and my prayer to God is sincere. -- Job 16:17.

When you pray, he will answer you, and you will keep the vows you made. -- Job 22:27.

Listen to my cry for help, my God and king! I pray to you, O Lord.

You hear my voice in the morning; at sunrise I offer my prayer and wait for your answer.

-- Psalms 5:2,3.

He listens to my cry for help and will answer my prayer. -- Psalms 6:9.

Listen, O Lord, to my plea for justice; pay attention to my cry for help! Listen to my honest prayer. -- Psalms 17:1.

But when they were sick, I dressed in mourning; I deprived myself of food; I prayed with my head bowed low. -- Psalms 35:13.

EVENING AND MORNING AND AT NOON, WILL I PRAY AND CRY ALOUD: AND HE SHALL HEAR MY VOICE. -- Psalms 55:17.

Because you answer prayers. People everywhere will come to you. -- Psalms 65:2.

I praise God, because he did not reject my prayer or keep back his constant love from me.
-- Psalms 66:20.

This is the end of the prayers of David son of Jesse. -- Psalms 72:20.

Hear my prayer; listen to my cry for help! -- Psalms 88:2.

He will hear his forsaken people and listen to their prayer. -- Psalms 102:17.

Pray for the peace of Jerusalem: "May those who love you prosper. -- Psalms 122:6.

The Lord is pleased when good people pray, but hates the sacrifices that the wicked bring him. When good people pray, the Lord listens, but he ignores those who are evil. -- Proverbs 15:8,29.

If you do not obey the law, God will find your prayers too hateful to hear. -- Proverbs 28:9.

When you lift your hands in prayer, I will not look at you. No matter how much you pray, I will not listen, for your hands are covered with blood. -- Isaiah 1:15.

You punished your people, Lord, and in anguish they prayed to you. -- Isaiah 26:16.

The Assyrian emperor has sent his chief official to insult the living God. May the Lord your God hear these insults and punish those who spoke them. So pray to God for those of our people who survive. -- Isaiah 37:4.

I will bring you to Zion, my sacred hill, give you joy in my house of prayer, and accept the sacrifices you offer on my altar. My Temple will be called a house of prayer for the people of all nations. -- Isaiah 56:7.

I cry aloud for help, but God refuses to listen. -- Lamentations 3.8.

By a cloud of fury too thick for our prayers to get through. -- Lamentations 3:44.

And I prayed earnestly to the Lord God, pleading with him, fasting, wearing sackcloth, and sitting in ashes. -- Daniel 9:3.

I went on praying, confessing my sins and the sins of my people Israel and pleading with the Lord my God to restore his holy Temple. -- Daniel 9:20.

When I felt my life slipping away, then, O Lord, I prayed to you, and in your holy Temple you heard me. -- Jonah 2:7.

Many peoples and powerful nations will come to Jerusalem to worship the Lord Almighty and to pray for his blessing. -- Zechariah 8:22.

THE PRAYER MADE IN FAITH WILL HEAL THE SICK. THE LORD WILL RESTORE THEM TO HEALTH, AND THE SINS THEY HAVE COMMITTED WILL BE FORGIVEN.

SO THEN, PRAY FOR ONE ANOTHER SO THAT YOU WILL BE HEALED. THE PRAYER OF A GOOD PERSON HAS A POWERFUL EFFECT.

Chapter XII

HOW TO USE THE MAGIC WORD, ALMIGHTY

Many people do not realize the power and the value in the spoken word, and that by vibrating the sound of their voice into the air it will return, bring an answer, and they will receive what they ask for. The Bible is full of evidence that God healed through the spoken word and that God created everything through the word. There is also evidence that the word was lost and was found. You may have lost it, or may never have found it, but you can learn how to use it and realize health, happiness and prosperity, providing that you use the word only for good, and do not use it in any way to injure others. The Magic Word, ALMIGHTY, must be used for blessing and not for cursing.

The Lord created the heavens by his command, the sun, moon, and stars by his spoken word. -- Psalms 33.6

When he spoke, the world was created; at his command everything appeared. -- Psalms 33:9.

Why won't God give me what I ask? Why won't he answer my prayer? What strength do I have to keep on living? Why go on living when I have no hope? Am I made of stone? Is my body bronze? What strength do I have to keep on living? Why go on living when I have no hope? -- Job 6:8,11,12,13.

What has happened before will happen again. What has been done before will be done again. There is nothing new in the whole world. Look," they say, "here is something new!" But no, it has all happened before, long before we were born. -- Ecclesiastes 1:9,10.

To everything there is a season, and a time to every purpose under the heaven:
A time to be born, and a time to die: a time to plant, and a time to pluck up that which is planted;
A time to kill, and a time to heal; a time to break down, and a time to build up;
A time to weep, and a time to laugh; a time to mourn, and a time to dance;
A time to cast away stones, and a time to gather stones together; a time to embrace, and a time to refrain from embracing;
A time to get, and a time to lose; a time to keep, and a time to cast away;
A time to rend, and a time to sew; a time to keep silence, and a time to speak;
A time to love, and a time to hate; a time of war, and a time of peace. -- Ecclesiastes 3:1-

From the above you have the proof from God's Word, the Bible, that there is power in the spoken word. Nothing changes and what has been will be, what has been done can be done. If God created by the spoken word, you can create through the use of the spoken word, and you can reach the universal supply through the Magic Word, ALMIGHTY, and receive everything you need to supply your wants and demands. There is a time and place for everything. This is a law laid down in the Bible. There are many references of going to the mountains to pray, of seeking a quiet, secret, peaceful place in which to pray. You can do no better than to follow the example in the Bible.

The Bible tells us that God is a spirit and that you meet God in the air. This is the reason you must use the spoken word and broadcast your prayer, or message, by putting it into the air. Man has within him the key to the process by which he may know all there is to learn and receive all that he needs from the universal, divine supply. You tune into this source and supply through the spoken word by putting your message in the air and the divine, universal mind, which is in tune with yours, will receive it.

Other men and women throughout the world who are in tune will receive your message and help you. You do not need any wires or any telephones to put your message or spoken word on the air so that it will reach throughout the world. You know that no wires are used with the radio, yet you know that all radios tuned to the same wavelength will receive the same message. This is one of the good reasons why you must not speak orally the wrong words or think the wrong thoughts, because they will be received by the minds in tune with yours and will be returned to you.

This is the law: that you reap just what you sow. You receive according to what you give or send out. It pays you to always start your prayers or the sounding of the Magic Word, ALMIGHTY, with blessings and love to others. That is what you want to return to you. The Bible tells us that it is not what goeth into a man's mouth that defiles him but what goeth out of his mouth that defileth him. Therefore, you must be guarded in your speech about others; do not criticize, condemn or find fault with others because the Bible says, as you measure to your neighbor, he will measure back to you. The Good Book also says: Judge not lest ye be judged. What right have you to sit in judgment of your neighbor or your fellowman. His acts are between him and his God. Vengeance is mine, saith the Lord. I will repay all.

When you know that you will receive according to what you send out you will then understand why you cannot afford to hate or think evil thoughts, because they will return to you. For your own good and for your own reward you must dwell on love and do kind deeds instead of injury to others. Remember, you cannot beat, evade, or cheat the Divine Law, and you will reap just what you sow. Now is the time to start sowing right and using the Magic Word, ALMIGHTY, to bring about good things for yourself and others.

The Time to Repeat the Magic Word

Based on the laws laid down in the Bible the best time to pray is morning, noon and night and this is the best time to use the Magic Word, ALMIGHTY. However, you may use it any time or place. In cases of emergency you call on God at any time for help and he gives you the blessings if you are living in obedience to the law. You should vibrate, chant or sing the Magic Word in three separate syllables.

First, vibrate AL (hold it as long as you can) so the vibrations reach your stomach and bowels and arouse the solar plexus and start it into action. The solar plexus is your superior brain. It gets you in tune with all the unseen forces and the supreme Divine Power. The solar plexus works while you sleep and heals your body and mind. Second, vibrate MIGH (sing or chant it) and hold the sound vibration as long as you can until you feel it in your stomach and bowels. Third, vibrate TY (sing or chant) as long as possible until you feel the vibration in the pit of the stomach and into the bowels. After you have completed singing or chanting the Magic Word, ALMIGHTY, it is now time to ask for what you want or need. Send your message into the air and then give thanks to God that you will receive what you have asked for. This is proving your faith in the Divine Power and the Magic Word.

You should also repeat and vibrate the following: I AM GOD, LOVE, which contains ten letters and ten is one of the Perfect numbers. The O in God, the O in Love means God, because the circle is all and contains all. It has no beginning and no ending. It is everlasting and represents the Divine Being. O, or the circle, includes the world and everything in it because it vibrates in a circle and takes in everything.

The Jews' name for God is YOD HE VAU HE, a word of four syllables containing ten letters or one of the perfect numbers. In ancient times the people understood how to use things not only on three plains but on the fourth dimension, which is one of the reasons the Jews used the name containing four syllables instead of three.

The word GOD contains three letters and I AM contains three letters. The word AUM also contains three letters and this is the word the Indians or Hindus use most to repeat, but the I AM is the one that the Almighty puts the great emphasis on:

"Then tell them that I AM hath sent you."

When you repeat I AM, sing or chant it, you attract or arouse the Divine Power and it benefits you. When you repeat I AM you are asserting your right as a child of God and are entitled to all the benefits, provided you obey all the Divine Laws. You cannot expect to receive all the good unless you act, work, give and express all of the good. Remember, you will reap just exactly what you sow!

Repeating

By repeating day after day the Magic Word, ALMIGHTY, singing, chanting or vibrating it, you will put your mind and body in tune with the Divine Power and will increase your hope and faith, and what you pray for will come to pass. Do not think that you can pray for one day, or one time, and expect to get results. You must obey the rule or law of the Bible: "Pray without ceasing." Repeat often: "The Divine Power is working through my mind and body day and night to perfect my mind, heal my body and bring an answer to my prayers." Work and have faith! When you have finished a prayer always repeat the word ALMIGHTY to close your prayer.

The best time to offer your evening prayer is just before going to sleep. At this time you are resorting to peace and quiet and it is more beneficial toward getting the best results. Thinking of others and praying for them just before going to sleep and sending out blessings to them, will help to bring blessings and benefits to you.

Mind and Body

The mind has a great effect upon the body. Doctors have found that many people who think they have a disease have nothing wrong with their bodies but have something wrong with their minds. It is usually all imagination. Psychiatrists have found that by getting people to confess or go over their past history they can locate the trouble, which is really a short circuit in the mind. You renew your mind and cleanse it when you forgive others and ask forgiveness yourself.

In this way you remove all the burdens and obstacles through the action of the mind, which affects your body. When your mind is renewed and cleansed of all evil thoughts or wrong imaginations, the body begins to heal and is transformed because the mind has been perfected. It is also possible that the body can be weakened by disease and this affects the mind. In most cases the main trouble is in the mind and when the mind functions properly, through the use of the Divine Power or Magic Word, ALMIGHTY, the body is healed.

When people are sick they get well because they believe they will. No man ever dies until he gives his consent to do so. As long as he has faith and holds on and believes in the power of the Divine Word he can prolong his life. Good health is a normal condition. It comes about by obeying all the Divine Laws and natural laws.

There are three kinds of laws or three applications of the one law. You must apply the spiritual law to spiritual things; the natural law or physical law to the body and to health; the law of finance to financial things. Yet the law is the same whether it be the spiritual, physical or financial: you reap just what you sow.

You might obey the spiritual law and at the same time disobey the law of health. In this way your mind might be at ease, but your body would become diseased. In the same way you might be obeying the spiritual and physical laws, having peace of mind and good health, but if you disobeyed the law of finance you would have losses. Strict obedience to all laws is what brings the reward.

Music and Sound

The Bible is full of proof of the power of sounds and of the spoken word. The Children of Israel were told to march around the walls of Jericho seven times in seven days and to sound the ram's horn. They obeyed this law or command and when the ram's horn was blown on the seventh day the walls fell down. This is the result of the natural law of sound, which can organize or build up or it can disintegrate and tear down.

A great violinist once said that if he could get the key to the Brooklyn Bridge he could tear it down through the sound of his violin. This is true. Glass can be broken to pieces by sound vibrations; the human body can be disorganized through unpleasant sounds. The body can be built up and healed through harmonious music or sounds.

Columbia University is teaching how to heal disease through music or sound. Anyone who has ever heard the scream of a panther knows that the sound will send cold chills down the spine and cause the hair to stand on end. The cause of this is that it disturbs the nerve center. The sound of the screech owl is so disturbing that it is difficult to sleep within hearing distance.

Everyone's body contains a harmonious keynote and when he finds what music soothes him he should listen, chant or sing it as often as possible. This will put the body in harmony and give peace and contentment to the mind.

During the last war, the Germans knew how to make sounds from the airplane to create fear in her enemy soldiers and almost paralyze their nerves so that they could not fight.

It has been said that music will tame the most savage beast. We know that the Hindus in India, through chanting, can tame the most dreaded of snakes, the Cobra, and when he is in perfect harmony through the sound of music he will not strike. Knowing the power of sound and the harmony of music you can understand what the result must be on your body and mind when you chant, sing or vibrate the Magic Word. It will produce harmony instead of inharmony.

Fear

You bring about fear because you do not understand God or the Divine Law. When you do understand these laws you are free and you do not fear.

Fear causes more trouble and misfortune than anything in this world. Job said: "I had a great fear and it came upon me." This proves that the wrong thoughts will bring about the wrong results. You must supplant fear with hope and faith. Learn how to use and apply the Magic Word, ALMIGHTY, which removes fear from your mind. Fear causes a short circuit in the mind and body, and until all fear is removed you cannot make progress.

Time

I spend the night in deep thought; I meditate, and this is what I ask myself. -- Psalms 77:6.

Shout for joy to God our defender; sing praise to the God of Jacob! -- Psalms 81:1.

You hear my voice in the morning; at sunrise I offer my prayer and wait for your answer.

-- Psalms 5:3.

The Lord is my strength and song, and is become my salvation. -- Psalms 118:14.

The above references tell you that it is good to sing or chant morning, noon or night, and to sing or chant aloud. This also means to sing or chant the Magic Word aloud.

Health and Healing

Apply the same rules of singing, chanting and vibrating the Magic Word, ALMIGHTY, for healing the body. Refer to the concordance and read everything in the Bible on fasting, breathing, eating, exercising, thinking and drinking water and bathing in water.

The three requirements to sustain life are: eating, drinking and breathing. Did you ever stop to think which is the most important and why? Men have fasted or gone without food for thirty to forty days and still lived and got well. One can seldom live without water for more than four days. Therefore, water is more essential than food. You cannot live four minutes without breathing. Just try holding your breath for one minute and see what happens. This is proof that proper breathing is the most important thing for your health and for your mind.

By vibrating the word ALMIGHTY, the Magic Word, you send the breath or the air to the solar plexus and to the bowels, thus putting the body in perfect harmony. This kind of breathing should be practiced three times a day: morning, noon and night, if possible. However, you can get results by doing it at any hour. Good results are especially received by practicing this just before going to sleep and when first awakening in the morning.

Take seven deep breaths, exhaling and inhaling, rest a few minutes between and take seven more deep breaths. Do this three different times, making twenty-one in all. However, seven times at one time will bring good results. Each time you exercise deep breathing, vibrate the three syllables of the Magic Word for three times and speak the words: "I want perfect health." If you have any special diseases or pains ask that they be removed. Speak the words: "I am sending the power of the Magic Word, ALMIGHTY, to my leg, stomach (wherever the pain may be)." Command the Divine Power through the Magic Word, ALMIGHTY, to go to the seat of your trouble and remove it. Have faith, believe that it will be done, and it will be done.

Eating

The problem of diet is different for different people. The Bible says that what is one man's food is another man's poison. Each of you must learn by experience what is best for you to eat. Moderation in eating is advisable. Most people eat too much. Read all references in the Bible under eating.

Water

This is next in importance to breathing. Most people do not drink enough water. You should drink water at least three times a day - morning, noon and night. It will help you if you drink water every hour, if possible. The body is over seventy percent water and you continue to lose water through perspiration and elimination and what is lost must be replaced.

Exercise

Stagnation is death and action is life. It is necessary to exercise in the open air as much as possible. Waking is generally recognized as one of the best forms of exercise. Correct breathing and exercising in bed is good. Each person can find the kind of exercise that will help him and suit him best.

Fasting

We have given many references on fasting as taught in the Bible. Everyone should practice it, both for the health and for mental condition. Fasting should be practiced at least four times per year at the change of the seasons. The time of fasting should be from three to seven days. Most people would be healthier and much better if they fasted one day in each week. Abstaining from food will not hurt you, especially for a limited length of time, but you must always drink plenty of water and breathe properly.

When you fast you give the stomach and bowels a rest and clean out all impurities. This removes the short circuit from the body and the mind, being very beneficial. Many chronic so-called diseases can be healed through fasting.

Things to Do to Bring Results

Give yourself to the Lord; trust in him, and he will help you.
Don't give in to worry or anger; it only leads to trouble. -- Psalms 37:5,8.
"Stop fighting," he says, "and know that I am God, supreme among the nations, supreme over the world." -- Psalms 46:10.
Morning, noon, and night my complaints and groans go up to him, and he will hear my voice. -- Psalms 55:17.
But as for me, I will pray to you, Lord; answer me, God, at a time you choose. Answer me because of your great love, because you keep your promise to save. -- Psalms 69:13.
Then men may know that thou, whose name alone is the Lord, art the most high over all the earth. -- Psalms 83:18.
Remember your promise to me, your servant; it has given me hope.
Even in my suffering I was comforted because your promise gave me life.
In the middle of the night I wake up to praise you for your righteous judgments.
Seven times each day I thank you for your righteous judgments.
Those who love your law have perfect security, and there is nothing that can make them fall.
I obey your teachings; I love them with all my heart. -- Psalms 119:49,50,62,164,165, 167.
Remember, when you learn how to use the Magic Word, ALMIGHTY, and obey all the laws and commandments of the Bible which will give you health, happiness and prosperity,

the one thing which you will have to guard against most is wrong speaking and wrong thinking. If you can overcome the greatest hindrance that brings about all others, which is fear, you will have accomplished all the results promised in the Bible through obedience to the Divine Law and through the use of the Magic Word, ALMIGHTY.

The Lord is my shepherd; I shall not want.

He maketh me to lie down in green pastures: he leadeth me beside the still waters.

He restoreth my soul: he leadeth me in the paths of righteousness for his name's sake.

Yea, though I walk through the valley of the shadow of death, I will fear no evil: for thou art with me; thy rod and thy staff they comfort me. -- Psalms 23:1-4.

This book, in order to benefit you, must not be read once and laid aside. Read it at least three times over a period of three weeks. Then read it one time each month in the year, and follow the instructions on how to use the word, ALMIGHTY, i.e., chanting, humming or saying the word.

HEART TROUBLE: MAN'S GREATEST ENEMY

Medical reports show that heart trouble is taking a greater toll of useful men and women each year than almost any other disease. Heart trouble can be cured through the use of the Magic Word, ALMIGHTY, and by proper breathing. All diseases can be cured by the divine power. The Bible makes this very plain. God's power is the greatest and best way. Try it and prove it to yourself.

THE END

***

W. D. Gann is in his 72nd year, he is in good health, active and young, and he can do as much work as he could when he was 30-years old. He gives credit to the divine power and by his using the Magic Word, ALMIGHTY, for his good health and success.

9 789650 060176